BUSINESS MATH

MATH 24/7

BANKING MATH

BUSINESS MATH

COMPUTER MATH

CULINARY MATH

FASHION MATH

GAME MATH

SHOPPING MATH

SPORTS MATH

TIME MATH

TRAVEL MATH

MATH 24/7

BUSINESS MATH

RAE SIMONS

Mason Crest

Mason Crest
450 Parkway Drive, Suite D
Broomall, PA 19008
www.masoncrest.com

Printed in the United States of America.

First printing
9 8 7 6 5 4 3 2 1

Series ISBN: 978-1-4222-2901-9
ISBN: 978-1-4222-2903-3
ebook ISBN: 978-1-4222-8914-3

The Library of Congress has cataloged the
        hardcopy format(s) as follows:

        Library of Congress Cataloging-in-Publication Data

Simons, Rae, 1957-
  Business math / Rae Simons.
      pages cm. – (Math 24/7)
  Includes index.
  Audience: Grade 4 to 6.
      ISBN 978-1-4222-2903-3 (hardcover) – ISBN 978-1-4222-2901-9 (series) – ISBN 978-1-4222-8914-3 (ebook)
  1. Business mathematics–Juvenile literature. I. Title.
  HF5691.S4329 2014
  650.01'513–dc23
                        2013015657

Produced by Vestal Creative Services.
www.vestalcreative.com

Contents

Introduction	6
1. Working: Earning Money	8
2. Working: Taxes	10
3. Working: Giving Change	12
4. Working: Checking Account	14
5. Working: Balancing a Checkbook	16
6. Starting a Business: Profit and Cost	18
7. Starting a Business: Office Area	20
8. Starting a Business: Loans	22
9. Starting a Business: Interest	24
10. Running a Business: Sales	26
11. Running a Business: Ordering Supplies	28
12. Running a Business: Discounts	30
13. Running a Business: Commission	32
14. Running a Business: Employees	34
15. Putting It All Together	36
Find Out More	39
Glossary	41
Answers	42
Index	46
About the Author	47
Picture Credits	48

INTRODUCTION

How would you define math? It's not as easy as you might think. We know math has to do with numbers. We often think of it as a part, if not the basis, for the sciences, especially natural science, engineering, and medicine. When we think of math, most of us imagine equations and blackboards, formulas and textbooks.

But math is actually far bigger than that. Think about examples like Polykleitos, the fifth-century Greek sculptor, who used math to sculpt the "perfect" male nude. Or remember Leonardo da Vinci? He used geometry—what he called "golden rectangles," rectangles whose dimensions were visually pleasing—to create his famous *Mona Lisa*.

Math and art? Yes, exactly! Mathematics is essential to disciplines as diverse as medicine and the fine arts. Counting, calculation, measurement, and the study of shapes and the motions of physical objects: all these are woven into music and games, science and architecture. In fact, math developed out of everyday necessity, as a way to talk about the world around us. Math gives us a way to perceive the real world—and then allows us to manipulate the world in practical ways.

For example, as soon as two people come together to build something, they need a language to talk about the materials they'll be working with and the object that they would like to build. Imagine trying to build something—anything—without a ruler, without any way of telling someone else a measurement, or even without being able to communicate what the thing will look like when it's done!

The truth is: We use math every day, even when we don't realize that we are. We use it when we go shopping, when we play sports, when we look at the clock, when we travel, when we run a business, and even when we cook. Whether we realize it or not, we use it in countless other ordinary activities as well. Math is pretty much a 24/7 activity!

And yet lots of us think we hate math. We imagine math as the practice of dusty, old college professors writing out calculations endlessly. We have this idea in our heads that math has nothing to do with real life, and we tell ourselves that it's something we don't need to worry about outside of math class, out there in the real world.

But here's the reality: Math helps us do better in many areas of life. Adults who don't understand basic math applications run into lots of problems. The Federal Reserve, for example, found that people who went bankrupt had an average of one and a half times more debt than their income—in other words, if they were making $24,000 per year, they had an average debt of $36,000. There's a basic subtraction problem there that should have told them they were in trouble long before they had to file for bankruptcy!

As an adult, your career—whatever it is—will depend in part on your ability to calculate mathematically. Without math skills, you won't be able to become a scientist or a nurse, an engineer or a computer specialist. You won't be able to get a business degree—or work as a waitress, a construction worker, or at a checkout counter.

Every kind of sport requires math too. From scoring to strategy, you need to understand math—so whether you want to watch a football game on television or become a first-class athlete yourself, math skills will improve your experience.

And then there's the world of computers. All businesses today—from farmers to factories, from restaurants to hair salons—have at least one computer. Gigabytes, data, spreadsheets, and programming all require math comprehension. Sure, there are a lot of automated math functions you can use on your computer, but you need to be able to understand how to use them, and you need to be able to understand the results.

This kind of math is a skill we realize we need only when we are in a situation where we are required to do a quick calculation. Then we sometimes end up scratching our heads, not quite sure how to apply the math we learned in school to the real-life scenario. The books in this series will give you practice applying math to real-life situations, so that you can be ahead of the game. They'll get you started—but to learn more, you'll have to pay attention in math class and do your homework. There's no way around that.

But for the rest of your life—pretty much 24/7—you'll be glad you did!

1
WORKING: EARNING MONEY

Ari just got his first job. He's out of school for the summer, and he wants to earn money for college. Ari applied for a job at a sporting goods store, and he got hired to work in the soccer gear department. He loves soccer, and he can't wait to talk about the sport with customers.

As part of his new job, Ari has a lot of tasks to do. He helps customers and tries to sell them things. He restocks the shelves in his department. He works at the cash registers sometimes.

One of the best parts about the job is the fact that Ari is earning money for the first time. He gets paid $9 an hour, which adds up fast because he's working so much during the summer. How much is Ari making?

Ari works for 30 hours every week. He knows he makes $9 an hour, so he can figure out how much he'll make per week.

$9 x 30 hours = $270 a week

How much money will he make over the whole summer? To find out, you'll need to count up the number of weeks in Ari's summer, which is nine. One of those weeks he'll be on vacation, though. So:

1. $270 x 8 =

Ari actually makes a little more money when he babysits his little sister. His mom pays him $10 an hour to convince him to babysit instead of hang out with his friends. So far, he has babysat these hours over the last month:

> Week 1—2 hours
> Week 2—4 hours
> Week 3—0 hours
> Week 4—2 hours

Ari is interested in how many hours, on average, he babysits, so he can guess what he'll make for the rest of the summer. Add up all the hours for the weeks, and then divide by the number of weeks.

2. What is the average number of hours Ari babysits his sister a week?

Now Ari can use the average to figure out how much he'll make babysitting over the summer.

3. How much money will Ari make babysitting? Remember, he has 8 weeks in his summer break.

4. How much money will Ari make in total during the whole summer?

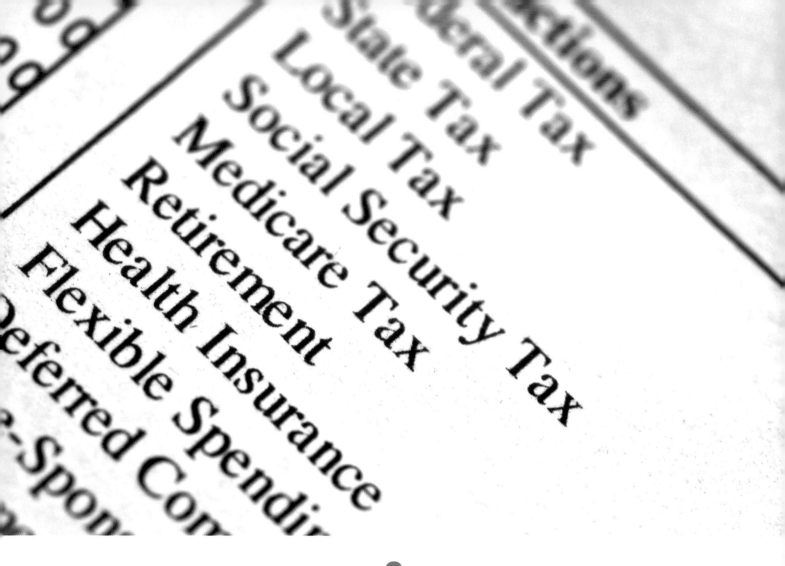

2
WORKING: TAXES

Even though Ari works 30 hours a week at $9 an hour, his first paycheck isn't for $270. He actually only got $206.14. What's going on?

The missing money went to pay taxes. The government collects money from everyone who works. The tax is called an **income** tax. The government uses taxes to pay for things like the police, schools, roads, bridges, and more. By paying taxes, you're actually helping to pay for all those things you use every day.

Ari can see at the bottom of his **pay stub** where the tax was taken out. He sees four taxes: federal income tax, state income tax, **Social Security** tax, and **Medicare** tax.

Someday Ari wants to own his own sporting goods store. He'll have to pay a lot of attention to taxes then, because business owners have to pay taxes on property (stores and land), on **income**, and on employees. Right now, though, Ari only has to worry about his own income tax.

Here are the different taxes and tax rates Ari had to pay:

Federal income tax: 10%
State income tax: 4%
Social Security tax: 6.2%
Medicare tax: 1.45%

Percents are parts out of 100, so 40 percent is 40 parts out of 100 parts. The problem with Ari's pay is that it's more than $100. Because he has earned $270, 40% of his pay would be more than just $40.

You can use cross multiplication to figure out how much each tax is. Try it for federal income tax:

$$\frac{10}{100} = \frac{X}{\$270}$$

$100 \times X = 10 \times \$270$
$100 \times X = 2700$
$X = 2700 \div 100$
$X = \$27$

You can also change percents into decimal numbers by moving the decimal point two spaces to the left. Now 10% becomes .10. Then you can just multiply the number you're starting with by the decimal. For federal income tax, you would get the same answer as before:

$0.10 \times \$270 = \$27$

Now do the same thing for the other three taxes.

1. How much does Ari pay in state income tax?

2. How much does he pay in Social Security tax?

3. And how much does he pay in Medicare tax?

4. Considering Ari will be making $206.14 every week at the store, after taxes, what will be his new total money earned for the summer?

3
WORKING: GIVING CHANGE

Part of Ari's job is to work at the cash register. Normally it's not very hard, and Ari gets to talk to a lot of people, which he likes. He scans the bar codes on the things people are buying, and the cash register adds it all up. Then the customer gives him the money (or a **debit card** or **credit card**) and he gives them change.

One day, the cash registers break! Ari's manager isn't about to close down the store, just because the system the registers use is broken. The cashiers can still open the cash register drawers, take money, and give people change.

Now Ari has to use his math skills to count up the money customers hand him and make sure it's enough. He also has to calculate the change he needs to give back, and he has to do it quickly.

The first customer in Ari's line is buying only one thing, a soccer ball. The ball costs $14.99, and the customer hands over a twenty dollar bill.

1. How much change should Ari give the customer?

The next customer's order is more complicated. Ari has to add up everything she's buying:

Sneakers, $51.50
Tennis racket, $129.00
Tennis balls, $2.59

2. What will the customer have to pay?

The customer doesn't have her debit or credit cards with her. She's going to pay in cash. She hands Ari a fifty dollar bill, six twenties, three dollar bills, and a quarter. He's never seen so much cash all at once!

3. How much did she give Ari? Did she give him enough money?

Ari counts up and tells her she hasn't paid enough. She gives him another twenty dollar bill and asks for her change. Ari does it in his head.

4. How much change will he give the customer?

4
WORKING: CHECKING ACCOUNT

Now that Ari is saving up so much money this summer, he wants to open up a checking account. He already has a savings account where he keeps all the money he's saving for college.

Checking accounts are where you can keep all of the money you are willing to spend. It's safer to keep money in a checking account rather than lying all over your bedroom floor or in your pockets. It's nice to have cash sometimes, but as Ari has discovered many times, you can lose it too.

Ari goes to the bank to set up a checking account. He talks to a bank employee, who tells him about the checking account the bank can offer him. He will have to keep at least $25 in his account at all times, or he will be charged a **fee**. He also has to use his debit card at least twice a month to keep his account active. Otherwise the bank might decide to close the account. He thinks he can do all that, so he signs up and puts $25 in his account. Now all he has to do is keep track of his money, and not spend too much! Check out the next page to figure out how Ari will manage his checking account.

Ari counts up all the money he has in cash at his house. He has a total of $48.83, which he takes to the bank and **deposits** in his checking account. Along with the $25 that's already in there, now he has $73.83.

The next day at work, Ari gets his first paycheck (for $206.14). He goes and deposits half of it in his account. He's saving the other half for college.

1.   Now how much does he have in his checking account?

Ari is really excited he has some more spending money. Now he can buy that new mp3 player he's been wanting. It costs $140.

2.   Does he have enough money? If so, how much money does he have left?

3.   Is the money left more than the $25 minimum he needs in his checking account to avoid a fee?

Ari is out with his friends when they all stop to get ice cream. He hasn't really been paying attention to how much money is left in his checking account, but he thinks he has enough to buy himself some ice cream. Then his friend Luisa asks if he can buy her a sundae and she'll pay him back later. Ari doesn't want to tell her no, so he agrees and spends a total of $12.50 on ice cream and other snacks.

4.   Does his checking account still have the minimum amount in it? If not, how low is it?

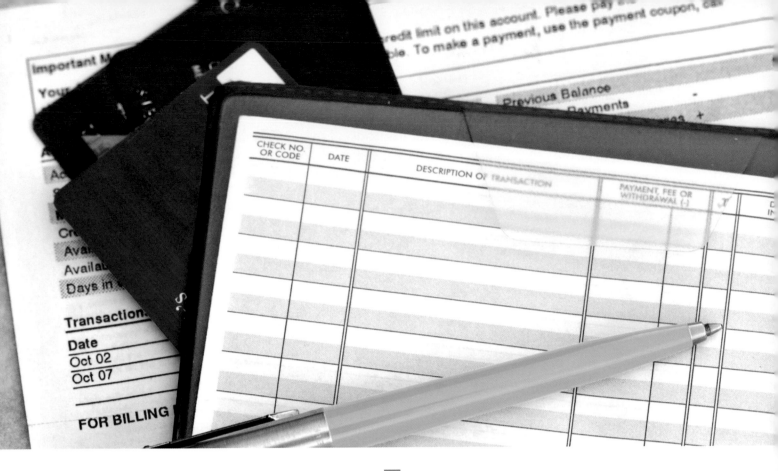

5
WORKING: BALANCING A CHECKBOOK

Ari is learning about managing money the hard way! After spending too much and paying the $30 fee for not having enough money in his checking account, he's paying a lot more attention to how he spends his money.

When he opened his checking account, Ari got a debit card and also a checkbook. He hasn't used his checkbook yet because he's not sure how. Right now, his uncle happens to be in town, and he sees the checkbook lying on Ari's desk. Uncle Elias tells his nephew he's going to teach him how to write a check and balance a checkbook.

Uncle Elias explains that Ari can check his checking account balance online. He can see what happens when he makes a purchase or a deposit. However, he should also keep track of his purchases and deposits in his checkbook. That way, if the bank or a store makes a mistake, Ari can catch it and make sure he isn't charged too much money. You can see what Uncle Elias teaches Ari on the following pages.

First, Uncle Elias asks Ari to gather together all of his receipts from stores and from making deposits at the bank. Here's what he puts together:

10/27—video game, $35.99
10/29—paycheck, $206.14
11/3—movie ticket, $11
11/7—babysitting money, $30

Now put all of Ari's receipts in the following chart. Purchases go in the withdrawal column, while money added to the account goes in the deposit column.

Date	Description	Withdrawal	Deposit	Balance
10/27	video game	$35.99	—	$74.37
10/29	paycheck	—	$206.14	$280.51

1. How much money does Ari end up with?

2. If Ari wrote a check for $300, would he have enough in his checking account to cover it? If so, how much does he have left? If not, how much more would he need?

The graph shows bars labeled **Sales** and **Costs** (with **Extra Costs** added on top of the Costs bar and crossed out).

6

STARTING A BUSINESS: PROFIT AND COST

Ari's older sister Eva is trying to start a business. She has always wanted to own a business, and now she's finally following her dream. Eva is starting a gardening business, because she loves growing plants.

Eva has already done a lot of planning. She knows she wants to start gardens in people's yards and even in pots on people's porches. She will provide the plants, the garden tools, and the other supplies. She will also teach people how to take care of their gardens.

She isn't sure how much she should charge her customers, though. She doesn't want to charge so much money that people won't be able to afford to hire her. She also wants to make money. Specifically she wants to make a profit, which is the money you make after you account for how much you had to spend to set up your business. How will she figure that out? You'll see how she decides what to charge her customers on the next page.

First, Eva lists all the things she'll have to spend money on to get a job done whenever she is hired. She will be offering two kinds of gardens at different prices— a garden in the yard, and a container garden on a porch, for people who don't have enough yard space or any yard at all.

In-ground garden:
Plants: $150
Compost: $40
Fertilizer: $6

Porch garden:
Plants: $115
Pots: $90
Dirt: $40
Compost: $10
Fertilizer: $6

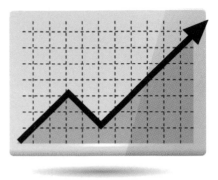

1. What are her total costs for each type of garden?

She could just charge her customers exactly how much it costs her to build a garden. But then she wouldn't make any money! She also has to account for how much her time is worth. She's putting in effort to start the business and build gardens, which is worth something.

Eva decides her time is worth $20 an hour, because she knows what she's doing and she'll be working hard.

2. If she plans on working an average of 8 hours on in-ground gardens and 3 hours on porch gardens, how much will she make at $20 an hour?

Now you can add the cost of building a garden to Eva's time, to get a good idea of what to charge customers. However, Eva also decides to add on some more money because she thinks customers will pay a little more. She adds $30 to the price of each garden. What should Eva charge customers who buy an in-ground garden?

$$\$196 + \$160 + \$30 = \$386$$

3. What about a porch garden?

Now you can find Eva's profit. You know how much it cost her to buy materials for each garden, and you know how much she is going to charge. The profit for the in-ground garden is the price Eva will charge minus the costs:

$$\$386 - \$196 = \$190$$

4. What profit will she make on the porch garden?

5. Which type of garden should she try to sell more of? Why?

7
STARTING A BUSINESS: OFFICE AREA

To start her garden business, Eva knows she wants to rent a small office. She'll be able to meet with customers, store documents there, and work on the computer from her office. Eventually she can even hire an employee to work in the office, once her business is doing well enough.

She shops around for a few offices. She knows she can only afford a small one, which is fine, because she'll be spending so much of her time outside planting gardens. At most, she can spend $500 a month on rent. Will she be able to find an office she can afford? The next page will help you decide.

The first office Eva looks at is $30 a square foot for the year, and it is 30 feet long and 15 feet wide. Can she afford it?

Here's the formula for square footage:

$$\text{Area (in square feet)} = \text{length} \times \text{width}$$

$$\text{Area} = 30 \times 15$$

1. Area of the office = _____ square feet

Now multiply the square footage by the rental price for the year and divide it by twelve months, to find the monthly rental cost.

2. Is it within Eva's budget?

Eva looks at a second apartment that is $18 a square foot for the year, and is 330 square feet.

3. Can she afford this one? Why or why not?

Eva needs space for two desks, three filing cabinets, and a table and chairs in her office. The desks are 3.5 feet x 1.5 feet. The filing cabinets are 1 foot x 1 foot. And the table and chairs take up 5 feet by 4 feet of space. And she wants to still be able to walk around, so she should have at least 100 square feet of extra room. Will this office have enough room for all of her stuff?

$$\text{Area of desks} = 2 \times (3.5 \times 1.5)$$

4. Area of desks =

5. Area of filing cabinets =

6. Area of table and chairs =

7. Now add up all the areas. Don't forget to take the walking space into account.

8. Does the office have enough room? If so, how much extra space does it have? If not, how much more space would it need.

8
STARTING A BUSINESS: LOANS

Eva doesn't quite have enough money to start her business. For example, she has to pay for wheelbarrows, hoses, and other garden tools. She also has to be able to buy the plants and pay the rent on her office for her first couple months in business. She thinks once she gets her business going, she'll be able to make plenty of money. First, though, she has to start making money. And businesses need money to make money.

Fortunately, Eva can get a loan from the bank. Loans are borrowed money. When she starts making money with the garden business, Eva will be able to pay the bank back.

Eva goes to the bank to ask about loans. She talks to a bank employee named Miguel about how much she should take out. Miguel takes her through some calculations. Help her figure it out on the next page.

Eva first has to come up with how much money she needs, so she can figure out how much in loans she should get.

Here's a list of all the expenses Eva will have to start her business:

first month's office rent: $495
wheelbarrow: $45.50
hoses: $19.99
pitchfork: $32.99
materials for first few gardens: $600
office supplies: $35
2 desks: $80 each
2 desk chairs: $48.75 each
3 filing cabinets: $17.50 each
table and chairs: $160.00
printer: 200.00
advertising: $50
gas for her truck: $60
business licenses: $150

1. How much will Eva need all together?

However, Eva won't need to borrow all that money. She has been saving up to start her business for a while. She has already spent some of it, but she has some left to pay for what she needs now that she's almost ready to open. In total, she has $600 saved.

The difference between the amount Eva needs to start her business and the money she has saved is how much she should take out in loans.

2. How much money should Eva get in loans?

STARTING A BUSINESS: INTEREST

While Eva is at the bank, Miguel also tells her about loan interest. Interest is the extra fee you have to pay just to take out a loan. You don't pay interest right away—you add it on to your loan payments when you start paying them back.

A high interest rate means Eva will have to pay a lot of extra money for her loan. A lower interest rate means she will have to pay less.

Miguel also explains that the loans the bank offers come with compound interest. Eva will be taking out $1560 in loans. Miguel tells her the bank's interest rate is 7.5%, and that she will have two years to pay off her loan. Her first interest payment will just be based on that original $1560 in loans. The second year, she will have to pay more interest. She will have to pay interest on the original loan, plus the interest she owes from the first year. The bank sees the interest as a second kind of mini-loan, so it charges interest on that. That's what "compound interest" means.

You can see interest can add up quickly! Check out the next page to find out how much Eva will have to pay in interest to take out a loan.

The math equation you use to calculate how much money you will have after interest is:

$$\text{total amount} = P\left(1 + r/n\right)^{nt}$$

That may look complicated, but it's not too bad once you know what all those letters mean.

P = how much money you are taking out, called the principal
r = the rate of interest, which the bank tells you; r is always a decimal.
n = the number of times interest is calculated over time. It might be calculated once a month or four times a year, or once a year.
t = the number of years you're looking at

The little nt is an exponent, which tells you how many times you will multiply a number by itself. 2^3 would be 2 x 2 x 2, which equals 8. Your calculator can do exponents for you.

Eva's information is:

P = $1560
r = 0.075 (from 7.5%)
n = 12, because interest will be calculated monthly
t = 2 years

Find the total amount of money Eva will owe, including interest, after two years:

1. Total amount = $1560 $\left(1 + .075/12\right)^{12\,x\,2}$

    Total amount =

2. How much of that total is interest?

item	jan	feb	mar	ap...			aug	sep	oct	nov	dec
P1032 R	524	499	485	464	544		...8	271	250	201	188
P1032 W	724	685	61...	661	799	70...		314	297	244	202
P1033 R	912	888						903	909	936	982
P1033 W	1112	1012					...47	1089	1123	120...
P1035 B									658	712	826
P1035 R									710	785	888
P1035 W									879	915	100...

10
RUNNING A BUSINESS: SALES

Now Eva has her business up and running. She has started advertising, set up her office, and is planting her first gardens for customers. Eva wants to keep careful records of her business, so she knows exactly what's going on.

She especially is interested in her sales, which is the money she's making from customers. The more customers she has, the more jobs she can do and the more money she can make. The first month of her business is a little slow, but by the second, she has a lot of customers.

Eva can calculate how much profit she's making, whether she's advertising well, and if she can make loan payments to the bank. Take a look at her records and see how much she's making in sales.

The first month, Eva has just three customers. She builds two in-ground gardens, and one porch garden.

1. How much does she make the first month? Look back to page 19 to see how much each garden costs.

At the beginning, Eva calculated how much she would charge each customer based on how much each garden cost to build. However, she forgot to include her monthly loan payments.

She has to pay $75 each month, in order to pay off her whole loan in two years. After the first month, she'll also have to pay rent and gas money.

She adds up the cost of building each of the gardens, and then adds it to her first month's loan payment. If it's less than the money she made this month, the difference is the profit.

2. Did Eva make any profit? If so, how much? If not, how much more did she need?

Her second month, Eva spends more time advertising. She ends up building five in-ground gardens and four porch gardens. But this month, she also had to pay for office rent and $60 worth of gas, plus the loan payment and the cost of garden materials.

3. Did Eva make a bigger profit this month than last, or did she make less?

11
RUNNING A BUSINESS: ORDERING SUPPLIES

Every time she gets hired, Eva has to order supplies to build a new garden. She works with her customers to figure out just what they want and what will work for their space. Some customers want flower gardens in their yard, some want bushes right outside the door, and some want vegetables in pots on the porch.

Eva is still figuring out what the best suppliers are. She likes to buy flowers from one supplier, vegetable seedlings from another, pots from another, and dirt from yet another. Sometimes she gets really confused about what is coming from where, but she knows it's important to keep track of it all.

To make sure she's paying the right amount of money, Eva always checks her order forms when her materials arrive. She has found mistakes a few times, so she knows it's worth taking the time to check.

Usually Eva fills out an order form that looks like this:

Date: 5/16
Order Number: 12345678

Description	Quantity	Price	Total
Squash seedlings	4	$3.99 ea.	$15.96
Tomato seedlings	5	$6.99 ea.	$34.95
Eggplant seedlings	3	$5.50 ea.	$16.50
Pea seedlings	10	$2.59 ea	$25.90
Radish seeds	1	$3 per package	$3
Lettuce seeds	1	$3.50 per package	$3.50

Total cost:	$99.81
Tax (8%)	$7.98
Shipping and handling	$6.54
Payment due	$114.33

What she actually gets is:

4 squash seedlings
4 tomato seedlings
0 eggplant seedlings
10 pea seedlings
1 package radish seeds
0 packages lettuce seeds

The company really messed up Eva's order!

1. What are the differences between the order form and what she actually receives by truck?

2. What is the price difference between what she ordered and what she got?

PRICE

12
RUNNING A
BUSINESS: DISCOUNTS

Eva is talking to her brother Ari about her business. She's been doing pretty well, but she wants a few more customers. She's been doing a lot of advertising, and she's not sure what else she can do to convince more people to hire her.

Ari has a great idea—he suggests she offer customers a discount. That way, the customers who thought Eva's prices were a little too high will decide they can afford a garden after all.

Eva agrees, and gets to work right away. On the next page, figure out how much of a discount she should advertise.

Eva will offer a certain percentage off her gardens. First she considers offering a 25% off coupon in the paper.

How much would 25% off be for a customer who ordered an in-ground garden?

You can calculate 25% off a couple different ways. First, you could think of the percentage in terms of fractions: 25% of something is the same as ¼ of something. So, for an in-ground garden, that costs $386:

$$\$386 \div 4 = \$96.50$$

Next, subtract the money customers will save from the total price of the garden:

$$\$386 - \$96.50 = \$289.50$$

You can also **convert** percentages into decimals. This means 25% would be .25. Then multiply the original cost by .25, and subtract that from the original cost. You'll get the same answer as before.

$$.25 \times \$386 = \$96.50$$
$$\$386 - \$96.50 = \$289.50$$

Now try it for the porch garden.

1. How much will customers pay if they get 25% off?

Eva only wants to offer a 25% off discount if she still makes a profit. Then she will still be making money, and also getting new customers who will tell their friends what a wonderful business she runs.

2. Will Eva make a profit off the in-ground garden if she offers a 25% discount? If so, how much of a profit will she be making after the discount? Turn back to page 19 for the numbers you need. Assume you don't need to take her monthly loan payment into account.

3. Will she make a profit from the porch garden? If so, how much?

4. Based on your answers, do you think Eva should focus on promoting 25% off on in-ground gardens or porch gardens?

13
RUNNING A BUSINESS: COMMISSION

Eva thinks her brother Ari is a good businessperson. She needs a little help now that her business is picking up, and she has a lot of customers. She asks Ari if he would want to work for her on commission.

She explains that commission isn't exactly like being hired. Instead, Ari will try to sell gardens to customers. Every time he sells a garden, he will earn a little money. The money he will earn is the **incentive** for him to work hard at selling gardens. The harder he works, the more money he earns.

Ari thinks it over and decides he wants some more money. He isn't working as many hours at the sporting goods store because he's back at school. By working on commission for his sister, he can choose what hours he works and still save up for college and get some spending money.

Employers can pay workers the same amount every time they make a sale. Or they can pay the worker a percentage of the sale, like 5% or 15%. The next page will show you how Eva figures out how much to pay Ari.

Eva will pay Ari a certain amount of money each time he convinces a customer to buy a garden. How much should she pay him for each garden?

She decides to pay Ari a percentage of her sales. She only sells two products, so it won't be hard to figure out how much she needs to pay him.

First, she tries out a commission rate of 1%.

What would 1% of an in-ground garden sale be? Use decimals.

1. .01 x $386 =

2. Do you think Ari would be wasting his time trying to sell gardens for that much commission? Does he have other choices that would allow him to make more money, considering it takes him two hours to make a sale?

   Eva sees paying a 1% commission is too little.

   Now calculate a 10% commission on an in-ground garden:

3. .10 x $386 =

4. What about a 10% commission on a porch garden?

5. How much would Ari make on an in-ground garden that was discounted by 25%?

   Ari decides a 10% commission sounds good to him, and he takes the job.

14

RUNNING A BUSINESS: EMPLOYEES

After just a few weeks, Ari brings in seven new customers to the garden business. Eva barely has time to keep up with all the new work, and she's starting to fall behind. Then she gets an idea—maybe she should hire her brother to work for her part time. He could do sales, and he could also help build the gardens.

Hiring an employee can cost a business a lot of money. On the other hand, her business can't grow if she can't do all the work. Ari has already made almost three hundred dollars working on commission, so she knows she can afford at least a few hours. She does a few calculations to see how many hours a week she can afford to hire her brother.

Eva knows she has to offer her brother at least the same amount of money per hour he is making at the sporting goods store. Otherwise, he has no reason to leave that job. So, she has to offer him more than $9 an hour.

1. How much would she be paying him a week if she paid him $11 an hour and hired him for 10 hours a week?

2. How much more would Ari make working for Eva than if he worked 10 hours at the sporting goods store?

Now Eva has to decide if she can afford to hire her brother for 10 hours a week, at $11 an hour.

She figures Ari will be working about four weeks a month, so she will pay him $440 a week. Eva also expects she'll be able to build more gardens with an employee's help. She **estimates** her business can build six more gardens a month.

Find the range of profits she could have. The range is the lowest possible profit to the highest possible profit. First, calculate what her profit would be if she builds six porch gardens, which make less profit. This is the bottom limit of the range. Turn to page 19 to find the profit numbers.

3. 6 x $90 =

Now do the math to find out if the six gardens were in-ground gardens, which make a higher profit. This is the upper limit of the range.

4. What is the upper limit of the range?

5. What is the range of profits she could make by hiring Ari?

6. Do you think hiring Ari is worthwhile? Why or why not?

15
PUTTING IT ALL TOGETHER

Eva ends up hiring Ari, and her business picks up even more. Eva's business is a success! She has come a long way from her first days starting the garden business. And Ari has come a long way from his first days working as an employee.

See if you can remember what Ari and Eva have learned about working and running a business.

1. If Ari were to get a raise to $13 an hour, how much would he make working 10 hours a week?

2. With the same tax rates he had before, how much would Ari's weekly paycheck actually have?

3. Ari puts 35% of his weekly paycheck into his checking account. How much does he have after 4 weeks, if he doesn't spend any of it?

4. Will Ari have enough money in his account if he deposits a $50 check his grandma gave him for his birthday—and then he buys a TV that costs $200?

5. The flower pots Eva usually buys for her customers suddenly go up in price. They are now $5 more each, and she usually buys 5 of them. How much will her profits be reduced by, if she doesn't raise the price of her gardens?

6. Eva's in-ground gardens are usually 6 feet by 8 feet. What is the area of the gardens in square feet?

7. How much would Eva have to pay each month on her loan if she only had a year to pay it off, and everything else was the same?

8. Eva is offering a new garden sale: every in-ground garden is 15% off. How much would one in-ground garden be?

FIND OUT MORE IN BOOKS

Benjamin, Arthur and Michael Shermer. *Secrets of Mental Math*. New York: Three Rivers Press, 2006.

Bernstein, Daryl. *Better Than a Lemonade Stand! Small Business Ideas for Kids*. New York: Aladdin, 2012.

Chatzky, Jean. *Not Your Parents' Money Book*. New York: Simon and Schuster, 2010.

Mooney, Carla. *Starting a Business: Have Fun and Make Money*. Chicago, Ill.: Norwood House Press, 2010.

Walsh, Kieran. *Money Math*. Vero Beach, Fla.: Rourke Publishing, 2004.

FIND OUT MORE ON THE INTERNET

Business for Kids
www.bschool.com/little-entrepreneurs-business-for-kids

Business Games for Kids
www.surfnetkids.com/businessgames.htm

Cool Math
www.coolmath.com

Money Instructor.com
www.moneyinstructor.com/business.asp

Teachingkidsbusiness.com
www.teachingkidsbusiness.com/business-basics.htm

Glossary

Compost: recycled plant materials that turn into dirt and are used to give plants extra food.

Convert: change into.

Credit card: a plastic card used to make purchases with small loans (credit).

Debit card: a plastic card used to spend money out of a checking account, instead of using cash.

Deposits: money put into a bank account.

Estimates: guesses.

Fee: money charged for the use of a service.

Incentive: a reason to do something.

Income: money you are bringing in.

Licenses: written permission to do something, usually given by the government.

Medicare: a government program that offers health care to the elderly and disabled.

Pay stub: the paper attached to a paycheck that explains how much tax has been taken out.

Rates: measures of how fast something happens.

Social Security: a government program that gives money to retired people.

Answers

1.

1. $2160
2. 2 hours
3. $10 x 2 hours x 8 weeks = $160
4. $2160 + $160 = $2320

2.

1. $10.80
2. $16.74
3. $3.92
4. ($206.14 x 8)+160 = $1809.12

3.

1. $20 – $14.99 = $5.01
2. $51.50 + $129.00 +2.59 = $183.09
3. No. She gave him $173.25.
4. $193.25 – $183.09 = $10.16

4.

1. $73.83 + ($206.14/2) = $176.90
2. Yes, he'll have $36.90 left over.
3. Yes.
4. No, he has $24.40, which is $0.60 less than he needs to have.

5.

1. $299.51
2. He doesn't have enough. He needs $25.49 more, including the money to the minimum balance that needs to be in his account.

Date	Description	Withdrawal	Deposit	Balance
10/27	video game	$35.99	—	$74.37
10/29	paycheck	—	$206.14	$280.51
11/3	movie ticket	$11	—	$269.51
11/7	babysitting money	—	$30	$299.51

6.

1. In-ground garden: $196, Porch garden: $261.
2. In-ground garden- $20 x 8 = $160, Porch garden- $$20 x 3 = $60
3. $261 + $60 + $30 = $351
4. $351 – $261 = $90
5. The in-ground garden, because she can make more profits.

7.

1. 450
2. No, it will cost $1125 a month.
3. Yes, it is $495 a month.
4. 10.5 square feet
5. 3 square feet
6. 20 square feet
7. Yes, it has plenty of space (10.5 + 3 + 20 + 100 = 133.5 square feet). It has 196.5 extra square feet!

8.

1. $2158.48
2. $2158.48 – $600 = $1558.48

9.

1. $1811.62
2. $1811.62 – $1560 = $251.62

10.

1. (2 x $386) +$351 = $1123
2. Yes, she made a profit of $395 her first month.
3. (5 x $386) + (4 x $351) = $3334
   $3334 – ($75 + (5 x $196) + (4 x $261) +$495 + $60) = $680
   She made $285 more in profit this month.

11.

1. 1 tomato seedling, 3 eggplant seedlings, and a package of lettuce seeds are missing.
2. $6.99 + $16.50 + $3.50 = $26.99

12.

1. $263.25
2. Yes, she will still make a $93.50 profit.
3. Yes, but only $2.25.
4. She should focus on discounting in-ground gardens, because she will make more money even with the discount.

13.

1. $3.86
2. He could be working at the sporting goods store or babysitting and making more money per hour.
3. $38.60
4. .10 x $351 = $35.10
5. .10 x $289.50 = $28.95

14.

1. $11 x 10 = $110
2. $20 more a week.
3. $540
4. $1176
5. $540 – $440 = $100 (lower limit), $1176 –$440 = $736 (upper limit)
6. Yes, because the business will make a profit no matter what.

15.

1. $130
2. $13 + $5.20 + $8.06 + $1.89 = $28.15, $130 – $28.15 = $101.85
3. 4 x (.35 x $101.85) = $142.59
4. No, he doesn't have enough to buy the TV.
5. $5 x 5 = $25.
6. 6 feet x 8 feet = 48 square feet
7. Total amount = $1560 $(1 + .075/12)^{12 \times 1}$
   Total amount = $1681.11
   $1681.11/12 months = $140.09
8. .15 x $386 = $57.90, $386 –$57.90 = $328.10

Index

advertising 23, 26–27, 30
area 20–21, 37
average 7, 9, 19

babysitting 9, 17
bank 14–17, 22, 24–26, 41
business 7, 10, 18–20, 22–24, 26, 28,
 30–32, 34–36

change 5, 11–13, 41
checking account 14–17, 37, 41
commission 32–34
costs 13, 15, 19, 27, 31, 37
customers 8, 12, 18–20, 26–28, 30–32,
 34, 37

debit card 12, 14, 16
decimals 31, 33
deposits 15–17, 37
discounts 5, 30

employee 14, 20, 22, 34–36
expenses 23
exponents 25

gardening 18

interest 24–25

job 8, 12, 18, 33–34
loans 5, 22–24

money 5, 8–19, 22–28, 31–34, 37

office 5, 20–23, 26–27

paycheck 10, 15, 17, 37
percents 11
profits 35, 37
purchases 16–17

rate 24–25, 33

sales 26, 33–34
supplies 5, 18, 23, 28

tax 10–11, 29, 37, 41

About the Author

Rae Simons is a well-established educational author, who has written on a variety of topics for young adults for the past twenty years.

PICTURE CREDITS